TURTLES

THE REPTILE DISCOVERY LIBRARY

Louise Martin

Rourke Enterprises, Inc.
Vero Beach, Florida 32964

Library of Congress Cataloging-in-Publication Data

Martin, Louise, 1955-
  Turtles/Louise Martin.

    p. cm. — (The Reptile discover library)
    Summary: Describes the physical characteristics,
behavior, and individual species of turtles.
    1. Turtles—Juvenile literature. [1. Turtles]
I. Title.
II. Series: Martin, Louise, 1955-
Reptile discovery library.
QL666.C5M27 1989   597.92-dc19   88-29709 CIP AC
ISBN 0-86592-578-X

Printed in the USA

TABLE OF CONTENTS

TURTLES

Turtles, tortoises, and terrapins are ancient creatures. They are grouped under the order name of Chelonia. Turtles first appeared two hundred million years ago, along with the first dinosaurs. They have changed very little since that time. There are two main kinds of turtles, Cryptodires (meaning hidden-necked) and Pleurodires (meaning side-necked). There are a total of about one hundred **species**.

A green turtle

HOW THEY LOOK

Turtles have leathery-skinned, fleshy bodies inside a hard shell. Their shells are in two pieces joined together on the underside. The rounded upper shell, or **carapace**, is made of bony plates fused together. The undershell is called the **plastron**. Turtles come in all shapes and sizes. Some species of turtles are tiny, and others can grow to over six feet long.

Florida box turtles have yellow marking on their carapace

WHERE THEY LIVE

Turtles can be found on every continent except Antarctica, in the far south. Some kind of turtles prefer **fresh water**, and others live in the ocean. Marine turtles are found in all the world's warm oceans. Some, like box turtles, live on dry land but enjoy wet conditions. They like the rain and sometimes soak themselves in muddy water for days.

Florida softshell turtles can be found in the Everglades in Florida

WHAT THEY EAT

Turtles can be **vegetarian** or **carnivorous**. Most have a mixed diet of fish, insects, shellfish, and water plants or seaweed. Snapping turtles also eat birds and small **mammals**. Green turtles are strictly vegetarian and feed mostly on seaweed. Vegetarian turtles are the best kind to eat. Carnivorous turtles sometimes eat dead animals, and that makes them taste bad.

An alligator snapping turtle eats a tadpole

Musk turtles give off smells when they feel threatened

Green turtles come ashore at night to lay their eggs

SNAPPING TURTLES

Snapping turtles have big heads and sharp, beak-like mouths. They are quick to attack with their powerful jaws. Snapping turtles snatch small mammals and birds from the banks of the pond or river. They drag them underwater and tear them apart to eat. Alligator snapping turtles *(Macroclemys temmincki)* are the largest freshwater turtles. They can weigh more than 150 pounds.

Alligator snapping turtles have strong jaws

GREEN TURTLES

Like all marine turtles, graceful green turtles are strong swimmers. Scientists recorded a green turtle swimming 300 miles in ten days. Green turtles are the only turtles known to **migrate**. A group of green turtles was seen nesting in the south Atlantic. Later the same turtles were found feeding close to Brazil. Those turtles swam nearly 1,500 miles from one place to the other.

Green turtles are very gracefu

NESTING

All turtles lay their eggs on land. Freshwater turtles make their nests in loose soil or fallen leaves. Ocean living turtles come ashore in the quiet of night to nest. They scoop out a hole in the soft sand and lay their eggs. The eggs are quickly covered over to protect them from **predators**. The females then leave the nest and return to water.

This green turtle is laying her eggs

BABY TURTLES

After seven to ten weeks the baby turtles hatch from the eggs. They fight their way out of the nest and head for water. Running down the beach or the river bank, the tiny turtles are attacked from all sides. Hungry birds, crabs, raccoons, and other animals swoop onto the defenseless turtles. Most of them are eaten up before they reach the water. Very few will complete a full life cycle.

Baby turtles have to leave the nest quickly and run to the sea for safety

TURTLES AND PEOPLE

Humans are among the turtles main predators. Hawksbill turtles' shells are used to make ornaments and jewelry. Many people all over the world eat turtle meat and turtle eggs. Green turtles are especially popular and have become quite rare. Now many countries have set up programs to help green turtles. No one is allowed to kill them or take eggs from the nesting grounds.

GLOSSARY

carapace (KARE a pace) — the upper shell of a turtle or tortoise

carnivorous (car NIV uh rus) — meat-eating

fresh water (FRESH WAH tur) — water found in lakes and rivers

mammals (MAM uls) — animals that give birth to live young and feed them with mother's milk

migrate (MI grayt) — to move from one place to another, usually at the same time each year

plastron (PLAS tron) — the undershell of a turtle or tortoise

predators (PRE duh turz) — animals that hunt other animals for food

species (SPEE seez) — a scientific term meaning kind or type

vegetarian (vej a TEAR ian) — an animal that only eats plants

INDEX